CW00739780

Benjamin Zephaniah Biography:

*Actor, Writer, and Poet Dies at Age 65/
Biography, Achievements, Facts About Him
and His Impact on the Poetry Space*

COLLETTE ALI

All rights reserved. No part of this publication may be reproduced, distributed, or transmitted in any form or by any means, including photocopying, recording, or other electronic or mechanical methods, without the prior written permission of the publisher, except in the case of brief quotations embodied in critical reviews and specific other noncommercial uses permitted by copyright law.

Copyright © Collette Ali, 2023.

Disclaimer

This autobiography of Benjamin Zephaniah is a work of admiration and extensive research by the independent publisher Collette Ali.

While efforts have been made for accuracy, some creative elements have been added. Benjamin Zephaniah and associates have not endorsed this work. It aims to inspire and celebrate her legacy.

Table of Contents

INTRODUCTION

Writer and poet Benjamin Zephaniah, who passed away at 65, is remembered as an influential figure in British literature.

His demise, attributed to a brain tumor diagnosis eight weeks ago, was confirmed through a statement on his Instagram, indicating that he was surrounded by his wife in his final moments. The announcement acknowledged the shared connection the world had with Zephaniah and anticipated the shock and sorrow felt by many over his passing.

Numerous tributes poured in, celebrating Zephaniah as a remarkable individual and a proud resident of Birmingham. Born and raised in Handsworth, Birmingham, to a Barbadian postman and a Jamaican nurse, his struggles with dyslexia led to his departure from school at the age of 13, unable to read or write. Moving to London at 22, he published his debut book, Pen Rhythm, which delved into dub poetry—a Jamaican art form later influencing the music genre of the same name. His association with The Benjamin Zephaniah Band and subsequent television appearances played a pivotal role in popularizing dub poetry in British households.

His literary contributions expanded to encompass novels, poetry for children and works like Talking Turkeys, a widely successful publication for younger readers. Zephaniah's multidimensional career spanned poems, literature, music, television, and radio, leaving behind a legacy celebrated for its joyous and impactful nature.

Beyond writing, Zephaniah showcased his acting prowess in the BBC drama series Peaky Blinders for nearly a decade. His refusal of an OBE in 2003 due to its ties to the British Empire and its historical association with slavery exemplified his staunch stand against colonialism and slavery, themes he often addressed through his work. His advocacy extended to racial abuse and education, rooted in personal experiences, including a criminal record from a past prison sentence for burglary.

His album "Rasta" and tribute to Nelson Mandela in the Wailers' first recording post-Bob Marley's death showcased his passion for social causes and political activism. Zephaniah's upbringing in a violent household shaped his early perceptions, where violence seemed normal until confronted by a friend's contrasting experience.

"This planet is for everyone, borders are for no one. It's all about freedom."

Benjamin Zephaniah

CHAPTER 1
BIOGRAPHY AND EARLY LIFE

Childhood

Benjamin Zephaniah was born on April 15, 1958, in Birmingham, England. He grew up in Handsworth, a culturally different area characterized by ethical pressures.

His nonage was marked by the challenges of poverty and ethnical demarcation. Living in a terrain replete with ethical pressure profoundly impacted his worldview and inspired his after-activism and poetry. Handsworth's rich artistic shade would later come as a vital source of alleviation for his cultural expressions.

Experience with Racial Discrimination and Identity Struggles

Zephaniah encountered pervasive ethical demarcation from an early age. These gests of prejudice and marginalization deeply affected his sense of identity. Growing up as a black child in a generally white society, he grappled with questions of belonging and plodded to find his place. These adversities fueled his desire to challenge societal morals and advocate for equivalency through his art.

Discovery of Poetry

Despite facing challenges in formal education, Zephaniah discovered his innate talent for poetry and writing at a young age. Writing became a cathartic outlet for him to express his thoughts, emotions, and experiences. His distinctive style, blending Jamaican Patois with traditional English, emerged during this period. Poetry became his medium for addressing social issues, voicing his concerns, and advocating for change.

Early Influences and Inspirations

Zephaniah's early influences were diverse, ranging from reggae music to the works of literary figures and political activists. He found inspiration in the works of writers who tackled social justice issues, such as Bob Marley and Langston Hughes. These influences shaped his artistic vision and encouraged him to use his voice to amplify the struggles of marginalized communities.

"Living rooms are arranged around the TV, but when you take away the box you have the freedom to arrange the room to suit yourself."

Benjamin Zephaniah

CHAPTER 2

LITERARY WORKS

Poetry collections: Themes, Styles, and Influences

Benjamin Zephaniah's poetry collections encapsulate a spectrum of themes resonating with social justice, identity, inequality, and the human experience. His verses often serve as a poignant commentary on racism, politics, and the complexities of society. Themes of empowerment, resilience, and hope are woven throughout his works, reflecting his commitment to addressing societal issues.

His style is notably distinctive, blending Jamaican Patois with standard English, creating a unique voice that bridges cultures and resonates with diverse audiences. This fusion of languages enriches the texture of his poetry, making it accessible while maintaining its authenticity. His rhythmic and engaging delivery, whether on stage or in written form, captivates readers and listeners alike.

Influenced by a myriad of sources ranging from reggae music to classic literature, Zephaniah's poetry is dynamic, emotive, and often thought-provoking. His ability to infuse his pieces with social commentary without compromising on the artistic depth sets his work apart and makes it both relevant and timeless.

Novels and fiction writing

Beyond poetry, Zephaniah has ventured into the realm of fabrication with novels that image his commitment to addressing societal issues. His novels explore themes similar to race, identity, and artistic clashes. With compelling narratives and pictorial characterizations, his fabrication jotting delves into the mortal condition, slipping light on the struggles faced by individualities in a different and frequently divided society.

These workshops serve as a platform to amplify marginalized voices, challenging compendiums to defy uncomfortable trueness about societal prejudices and systemic shafts. Zephaniah's liar prowess in fabrication glasses the same passion and social knowledge apparent in his poetry, witching compendiums while provoking soul-searching and discussion.

Children's literature and contributions to young readers

Zephaniah's fidelity to engaging youthful minds led him to contribute significantly to children's literature. His books for youthful compendiums attack themes of diversity, acceptance, and commission. Through engaging narratives and relatable characters, he encourages children to embrace their oneness and celebrate differences. His stories not only entertain but also disseminate important values of empathy, kindness, and understanding.

His capability to address complex issues in a manner accessible to children makes his benefactions to children's literature inestimable in shaping youthful minds and fostering a more inclusive generation.

Use of language and dialect in his works

A hallmark of Zephaniah's erudite style is his artfulness in using language and shoptalk to produce a rich and different shade of expression. His objectification of the Jamaican language and colorful cants in his jotting breaks conventional verbal walls, inviting compendiums into a world where language becomes an important vehicle for artistic emulsion and understanding. This skillful manipulation of language not only enriches his work but also serves as a testament to the inclusivity and diversity he advocates for in society.

CHAPTER 3
ACTIVISM AND ADVOCACY

Social justice campaigns and activism

Benjamin Zephaniah is famed for his unvarying commitment to social justice causes. He laboriously engages in juggernauts and enterprises aimed at addressing societal inequalities and promoting inclusivity. Through his art and public presence, he lifelessly advocates for marginalized communities, challenging systemic walls to equivalency.

Zephaniah's involvement in colorful social justice juggernauts spans issues like poverty, homelessness, LGBTQ rights, and access to education. His activism extends beyond words, as he laboriously participates in movements seeking for palpable societal change.

Advocacy for human rights and racial equality

Zephaniah's advocacy for mortal rights and ethical equivalency forms a foundation of his activism. He vehemently speaks out against ethnic differentiation and inequality, drawing from his particular gests to amplify the voices of those facing analogous challenges.

His sweats to strike prejudices and promote ethnical harmony are apparent in his jottings, speeches, and engagements with communities. Through his important advocacy, Zephaniah aims to produce a more just and indifferent society where individuals of all races and backgrounds are treated with quality and respect.

Environmental activism and sustainability efforts

Zephaniah's commitment to environmental activism and sustainability underscores his holistic approach to social change. He raises mindfulness about environmental issues, emphasizing the interconnectedness of environmental health and social justice. His advocacy encourages sustainable living practices and highlights the urgency of addressing climate change. Zephaniah's active involvement in environmental juggernauts showcases his belief in the significance of conserving the earth for unborn generations, incorporating his passion for social justice with environmental activism.

Anti-racism initiatives and participation in protests

A staunch advocate for anti-racism initiatives, Zephaniah is actively involved in protests and movements aimed at combatting racism in all its forms. He uses his platform to confront systemic racism and its detrimental effects on individuals and communities.

His participation in protests serves as a powerful call to action, inspiring others to join the fight against racial injustice. Zephaniah's advocacy work in anti-racism initiatives extends beyond conventional activism, penetrating the realms of literature and education, where he strives to foster a deeper understanding of racial equality.

"Nothing is as it seems. Seeing is not believing. Sometimes... you have to feel, touch, experience... and use your intelligence."

Benjamin Zephaniah

CHAPTER 4

ARTISTIC ENDEAVORS

Music collaborations and albums

Zephaniah's artistic journey extends into the realm of music, where he collaborates with musicians, infusing his poetic verses into compelling rhythms. His music albums serve as a fusion of poetic storytelling and musical expression.

Collaborations with reggae artists and musicians amplify his powerful messages, reaching audiences through a different medium. The synergy between his poetry and music creates a captivating experience, resonating with listeners and enhancing the impact of his socially conscious themes.

Performances: stage, television, and spoken word

Zephaniah's magnetic stage presence and captivating performances have left a lasting impression on audiences worldwide. Whether on stage, on television, or through spoken word presentations, his delivery exudes passion and conviction. His performances transcend mere recitations; they are emotive, engaging, and often thought-provoking. His ability to command attention and evoke powerful emotions through his spoken word artistry showcases his talent as a captivating performer, leaving a lasting impact on those who experience his live performances.

Multifaceted artistic expressions beyond poetry

Beyond poetry and music, Benjamin Zephaniah's artistic repertoire encompasses a wide array of expressions. He explores various mediums such as acting, painting, and storytelling. His ventures into these diverse artistic forms showcase his creative versatility and a deep-rooted passion for artistic expression beyond the written word. These endeavors demonstrate his commitment to using different platforms to convey his messages of social justice and equality.

Influence of music on his poetry and activism

Music plays a vital part in shaping Zephaniah's poetry and activism. The metrical meter and emotional depth of music influence the tone and delivery of his poetry, enhancing its impact. The emulsion of music and poetry allows him to connect with the cult in a visceral position, amplifying the resonance of his dispatches. Similarly, music serves as an important tool in his activism, enabling him to reach a wider cult and enkindle exchanges about social change through a medium that transcends language walls.

"Rap comes from the oral tradition. The oral tradition gives voice to those who would've otherwise been voiceless."

Benjamin Zephaniah

CHAPTER 5
PERSONAL BELIEFS AND CHOICES

The decision to decline an OBE

In 2003, Benjamin Zephaniah declined an Order of the British Empire(OBE), a prestigious honor, citing his expostulation to the social history and heritage of the British Empire. His turndown to accept the award was a bold statement against the shafts and atrocities executed during the period of British colonialism.

Zephaniah's decision was embedded in his unvarying principles and commitment to standing against literal shafts, indeed at the cost of particular recognition. This bold act garnered attention and sparked conversations about the complications of public honors and the significance of particular integrity in the face of systemic shafts.

Commitment to principles and values

Zephaniah's life and work are deeply entrenched in his principles and values. His steadfast commitment to social justice, equality, and human rights is evident in every facet of his activism and artistic endeavors. His principles serve as a moral compass, guiding his actions and decisions, whether in declining prestigious honors or actively engaging in advocacy for marginalized communities. His unwavering dedication to his values reinforces his credibility as an advocate for positive social change.

Influence of personal experiences on his beliefs and activism

Zephaniah's particular gests, particularly growing up in Handsworth and facing ethical demarcation, significantly shaped his beliefs and activism. These gests of marginalization and injustice fueled his passion for championing systemic inequalities. His immediate hassles with societal prejudices and rigors became driving forces behind his commitment to addressing social issues, giving voice to the marginalized, and challenging the status quo.

Integration of beliefs into his artistic and personal life

The integration of his beliefs into both his artistic and personal life is a defining aspect of Zephaniah's character. His art serves as a powerful medium to express and amplify his beliefs, acting as a catalyst for societal change.

Whether through his poetry, music, or other artistic pursuits, his commitment to social justice remains at the forefront, interwoven into the fabric of his creative expressions. Moreover, his personal life reflects his principles, as he lives authentically by the values he espouses, staying true to his convictions even in the face of societal pressures or expectations.

"School was preparation for the future... and he had no intention to go into the future unprepared."

Benjamin Zephaniah

CHAPTER 6

IMPACT AND LEGACY

Global influence and reach of his works

Benjamin Zephaniah's erudite and activist trials have transcended borders, reverberating with cult encyclopedically. His poetry, music, novels, and advocacy work have reached different communities, inspiring individualities across the mainland.

His universal themes of social justice, equivalency, and commission strike a passion with people from colorful artistic backgrounds, fostering connections and sparking exchanges about important societal issues. Zephaniah's capability to allure hearts and minds around the world underscores the global impact of his workshop, leaving an unforgettable mark on erudite and artistic geography.

Contributions to literature and the arts

Zephaniah's contributions to literature and the arts are immeasurable. His body of work spans poetry collections, novels, children's literature, and music albums, showcasing his versatility as an artist. Through his powerful storytelling, he challenges societal norms, amplifies marginalized voices, and prompts critical reflections on pressing social issues. His fusion of language, his unique style, and his ability to provoke thought through his artistry have significantly enriched the literary and artistic spheres, leaving an enduring legacy for generations to come.

Inspiring future generations and aspiring writers

Zephaniah's impact extends beyond his cultural achievements; he serves as an alleviation for unborn generations and aspiring pens. His trip from a grueling background to becoming a prominent erudite figure resonates with individualities facing analogous obstacles.

His authenticity, adaptability, and fidelity to social causes serve as a lamp of stopgap, encouraging aspiring pens to use their voices for positive change. Through mentorship, public engagements, and advocacy for creative expression, Zephaniah inspires rising bents to valorously pursue their heartstrings and contribute meaningfully to society.

Enduring legacy in social justice movements.
Zephaniah's impact extends beyond his cultural achievements; he serves as an alleviation for unborn generations and aspiring pens. His trip from a grueling background to becoming a prominent erudite figure resonates with individualities facing analogous obstacles.

His authenticity, adaptability, and fidelity to social causes serve as a lamp of stopgap, encouraging aspiring pens to use their voices for positive change. Through mentorship, public engagements, and advocacy for creative expression, Zephaniah inspires rising bents to valorously pursue their heartstrings and contribute meaningfully to society.

"The way animals are carted around reminds me of the slavery of my people... The slavery of animals has to be ended too."

Benjamin Zephaniah

CONCLUSION

Benjamin Zephaniah, a titan of British literature, leaves an indelible mark on the world as a revered writer, poet, musician, activist, and cultural icon. His life's journey, shaped by experiences of racial discrimination, identity struggles, and societal injustices, became the canvas upon which he painted powerful narratives through his poetry, literature, and activism.

Born and raised in Handsworth, Birmingham, Zephaniah's early years were marked by challenges, including leaving school at 13, dyslexia, and encounters with the racial prejudices of the era. Yet, these experiences became the bedrock of his artistry, driving him to explore the realms of poetry and writing as a means of self-expression and social commentary.

Zephaniah's literary works stand as testaments to his creative prowess and commitment to social justice. His poetry collections, novels, and children's literature reflect diverse themes, styles, and linguistic innovation, showcasing his ability to captivate audiences while addressing pressing societal issues.

Beyond his literary contributions, Zephaniah's advocacy and activism have been catalysts for change. His unwavering stance against injustice, reflected in his environmental activism, anti-racism initiatives, and human rights advocacy, resonates globally, inspiring generations to stand up against oppression and inequality.

His artistic endeavors expanded beyond poetry, encompassing music collaborations, stage performances, and television appearances, amplifying his message of social change and unity across various mediums. The fusion of music with his poetry not only enriched his artistic expression but also bolstered his activism, resonating with diverse audiences.

Zephaniah's personal beliefs, epitomized by his principled rejection of an OBE due to his stance against empire, reflected his unwavering commitment to his values. His integrity, rooted in personal experiences and convictions, transcended accolades, intertwining seamlessly with his artistic and activist endeavors.

As a global influencer, Zephaniah's legacy extends far beyond literature and the arts. His contributions to social justice movements, his tireless advocacy for equality, and his ability to inspire and empower future generations of writers, activists, and dreamers solidify his enduring impact.

In conclusion, Benjamin Zephaniah's life and work resonate as a testament to the power of art, the strength of conviction, and the unwavering spirit of activism. His legacy as a literary luminary and a fearless advocate for change continues to echo through time, shaping not only the world of literature and activism but also the hearts and minds of those who champion justice, equality, and the power of words.

Printed in Great Britain
by Amazon

35081995R00030